HAMPTONS GARDENS

A 350-YEAR LEGACY

HAMPTONS GARDENS

A 350-YEAR LEGACY

JOHN ESTEN

NEW PHOTOGRAPHS BY
EVELENE WECHSLER

PUBLISHED IN CONJUNCTION WITH THE EXHIBITION
ORGANIZED BY THE GUILD HALL MUSEUM, EAST HAMPTON, NEW YORK

Alfonso Ossorio's was an enigmatic landscape garden of contradiction and surprise.[1]
—LESLIE ROSE CLOSE

In 1952, artist Alfonso Ossorio bought an Italianate house and an almost sixty-acre property called The Creeks on the northern shore of Georgica Pond in East Hampton. For the next forty years of his life, Ossorio created a vast parklike garden of rare conifers intermingled with native trees and shrubs that became a living work of art or, as the artist called it, "his ultimate congregation." Photographer Linda Alpert framed part of Ossorio's "congregation" in November 1990.

ENDPAPERS:
A garden plan for the Neil Hirsch estate in Water Mill, by landscape designer Jack Whitmore.
A photograph of the garden appears on pages 100-101.

OPPOSITE TITLE PAGE:
WALTER COLE BRIGHAM, *Up the Brick Walk, Late Afternoon*, ca. 1935.
Soon after he completed his studies in New York and Florence, Brigham returned to Shelter Island where he set up a studio overlooking Dering Harbor. *Up the Brick Walk* is one of several paintings the artist made of the garden at Sylvester Manor.

First published in the United States of America in 2004 by
Rizzoli International Publications, Inc.
300 Park Avenue South
New York, NY 10010
www.rizzoliusa.com

Library of Congress Control Number: 2003116895

ISBN: 0-8478-2617-1

CREDITS:
Book design: John Esten
Digital Composition: Mary McBride
Printed in China

CONTENTS

High above the beach in East Hampton, a splashing water nymph surveys the pool and enclosed sunken garden below the Elizabethan-style house, built in 1918.

FOREWORD/ ACKNOWLEDGMENTS

WHEN THE DISCOVERERS and explorers of the New World stepped ashore, they were confronted with a vast, natural garden abundant with trees, plants, and other curious wonders. These intrepid people were curious and eager to observe the unknown Eden.

"Arcadia" is how the great navigator Giovanni da Verrazano described the landscape he initially encountered in the summer of 1524. This Italian, who was the first European to view Long Island, later recorded enthusiastically that, "we found wild roses, violets, and lilies, and many kinds of herbs and fragrant flowers," describing further that what he had seen was "different from ours" back home.

More than a century later, other intrepid people stepped ashore on the easternmost end of Long Island and were equally in awe of the unspoiled paradise they found flourishing there, and immediately planted gardens that created a legacy that continues to this day.

The more than year-long preparation of this book and exhibition has been an unmitigated pleasure. Imagine spending one's time looking at other people's gardens, pictures, and photographs and never having to feel a twinge of guilt about not having to clock into an office every day! However, the longer a project of this sort is in preparation, the more people there are to thank and the greater the chance that someone may be overlooked.

Unlike most photographers, Evelene Wechsler, who photographed the new images for the exhibition and book, serenely and swiftly went about her work producing these wonderful pictures. I know, Evey, the days we got rained on or the one when you cracked your wrist didn't seem so serene.

I am indeed indebted to the professional assistance of individuals associated with museums, libraries, and other institutions: Betsy Feeley, American Academy of Arts and Letters; Jeffrey Fleming and Nora Cammann, Bridgehampton Historical Society; Diana Dayton and Dorothy King, Long Island Collection, East Hampton Free Library; David Rattray, Robert Long, and Alice Ragusa, *East Hampton Star*; Judy Sourakli and Ife Williams, Henry Art Gallery, University of Washington; Matko Tomicic and Wendy Van Deusen, LongHouse Reserve; Deanna Cross, Metropolitan Museum of Art; Mildred De Riggi, Nassau County Museum; Alicia Longwell and Chris McNamara, Parrish Art Museum; Helen Harrison, Pollock-Krasner House and Study Center; Louise Tuthill Green, Shelter Island Historical Society; Joyce Connolly and Beth Page, Horticultural Services Division, Archives of American Gardens, Smithsonian Institution; Richard Barons, Southampton Historical Museum.

Owners of artworks, dealers, and auction houses who helped me locate and borrow specific paintings for the exhibition and provide materials to reproduce in this book are: Dorsey Waxter, Artemis; Greenberg Van Doren Gallery; Arlene Bujese, Arlene Bujese Gallery; David Beausoleil, Denise Bibro Fine Art; Mason Thune, Christie's; Eric W. Baumgartner, Hirschl and Adler Gallery; Arnie and Elizabeth Tops Lizan and Pamela Williams, Lizan Tops Gallery; Betty Cunningham and Gard and Nina Madison, Robert Miller Gallery; Eric Brown, Tibor de Nagy Gallery; Terry Wallace, Wallace Gallery; and Francis H. Williams.

Among others who have assisted me are: Alice Fisk, Jeremiah Goodman, Robert J. Hefner, John Hill, Pamela Lord, Joan Ludman, Ruth Mueller, Ruth Nivola, and Robert Wechsler.

I would also like to thank Elizabeth Parella, who compiled the index and initally edited my text, and Eva Prinz, my editor for its final edit, who provided her support throughout the many aspects of this project. I am grateful to Charles Miers, publisher of Rizzoli International Publications, whose insight and enthusiasm made an idea a reality. Jacquie Byrnes, production manager for Rizzoli, was equally supportive.

I am indebted to Mary McBride for her expertise and diligence in converting my words and layout design into a computer format to make this book.

I especially want to thank Ruth Applehof, director of the Guild Hall Museum in East Hampton, for enabling an idea to materialize on the walls of the museum. Working with Christina Strassfield, curator of the museum, her associate Maura Doyle, and the Guild Hall staff has been a continuous pleasure. Indeed, "Who could ask for anything more?" □

When Leo Revi painted *July Garden, The Circle,* in 1976, he found inspiration close by in the garden outside his front door erupting with brilliant blossoms, just steps from Main Street in East Hampton.

Shortly after he came to East Hampton in the early summer of 1898, Childe Hassam painted a flower-filled garden directly in front of one of the town's eighteenth-century heirloom-shingled cottages that he called *Old House and Garden, East Hampton, Long Island.*

HAMPTONS GARDENS
A 350-YEAR LEGACY

Half the fun of a garden is showing it to someone else...[2]

—RUTH DEAN

ADRIAN VAN DER DONCK, one of the nine men who governed New Amsterdam, came to the Dutch settlement in 1642 and purchased a "bouwerie" or large estate (now Yonkers) above Manhattan and gave the first comprehensive account of the gardens, flowers, fruits and vegetables in his adopted land. Writing in *A Description of the New-Netherlands,* published in 1655, he recorded that "[a] certain chirurgeon who was also a botanist, had a beautiful garden there, wherein a great variety of medicinal and wild plants were collected..." Along with describing the town and topography of New Amsterdam, he enthusiastically exclaimed that "Long Island, which on account of its fine bays and havens, and good lands, is a *crown of the Province.*"

Just two years before the Dutch chronicler arrived at the western end of Long Island, a group of settlers had put down roots on the eastern end. Among the meager possessions these intrepid offspring of New England Puritans carried with them on their journey across Peconic Bay were seeds, roots, and cutting-slips they quickly planted in enclosed gardens to help ensure their survival.

Gardens had been planted and vigilantly tended by the Algonquin peoples on Long Island about ten centuries before Columbus arrived to the New World. According to historian John A. Strong, "eastern Algonquian Indians marked the beginning of the planting season when the [constellation] Pleiades, a bright cluster of stars, completed its winter trek cross the sky and disappeared in the west during the first week in May."[3] Gardening was always the province of women, who propagated corn, beans, pumpkins, and squash in cleared plots of one-half to two acres adjacent to their villages. Strong further points out that tobacco "was in the male domain. The men planted, tended, and harvested the sacred plant, which was generally grown in a separate area some distance away from the other crops."[4]

The fenced-in gardens the transplanted Puritans established were situated close to their new homes, laid out as a direct route from their front or back doorways for easy access to care for their precious plants. The gardens were divided into rectilinear beds according to the Elizabethan gardens cultivated back in England. The beds were often raised by building up the soil, which was held in place by stakes interwoven with twigs or saplings, called wattles. The walks between the beds were usually tamped soil, gravel, or crushed oyster or clam shells. The gardens were completely functional, combining familiar vegetables and herbs that supplied both pantry and medicine chest. One of the first chroniclers of gardening in America, William Wood, came to New England in 1629 and four years later published the *New England Prospect*, in which he observed:

The ground affoards very good kitchin gardens, for Turneps, Parsnips, Carrots, Radishes, and Pompions, Muskmillons, Isquoter-squashes, coucumbers, Onyons, and whatever grows well in England grows as well there, many things being better and larger: there is likewise growing all manner of Hearbes for meate and medicine...

[such as] sweet Marjoran, Purslane, Sorrell, Peneriall, Yarrow, Mirtle, Saxifarilla, Bayes, etc.[5]

The Southampton saltbox home, built by Thomas Halsey in 1660 and now the oldest house on the South Fork of the island has a re-created garden that is a partial example of an early dooryard garden. Another re-created dooryard garden is in front of the Mulford house on James Lane in East Hampton, built about 1680 and acquired by Samuel Mulford in 1698. The foursquare garden with raised beds simulates a garden planted by Rachel Mulford in 1790.

Another island enriches the history of gardening on the East End of Long Island. Nestled in the V of the moraines between the North and South Forks, the Shelter Island garden at Sylvester Manor is one of the earliest extent gardens in North America.

A member of a wealthy English family with ties to the ill-fated King Charles I, Nathaniel Sylvester purchased the entire island from William, Earl of Sterling, in 1637. After the monarchy fell, Sylvester came to Shelter Island on his wedding trip in 1653.

Landscape designer Edwina van Gal looked back to medieval wattles when she surrounded the rectangular beds at Coxwould, Lowell Schulman and Dianne Wallace's rose garden on Lily Pond Lane in East Hampton.

There he built a manor house for his sixteen-year-old bride and planted boxwood cuttings (presumably *Buxus sempervirens,* now called American box) that the couple had brought with them which still survive in the remnants of their original garden. (By Sylvester family tradition, box hedges are decorated with gold leaf when the heir of the manor brings home a new bride.)[6] To this day the garden at Sylvester Manor has a continuous history of cultivation by descendants of the family and has inspired American gardeners and horticulturists throughout succeeding centuries.

On Long Island, blessed with the rich glacial humus deposited fifteen or more millennia ago, almost any plant will thrive. Writing in *Beautiful Gardens of America* in 1915, Louise Shelton commented on the "marked softness of the winter climate especially near the sea." She explained further that Southampton "in proportion to [its] population has probably a greater number of gardens than any town in the State, many of them designed and developed by their owners, who have thus delightfully expressed their love for flowers."

One of the Southampton gardens Louise Sheldon included in her book was The Orchard (today called Whitefield), a large formal garden defined by brick, herringbone-pattern walks and a Doric pergola surrounding its three sides, directly behind the colonial revival-style mansion designed by McKim, Mead, and White in 1906 for Mr. and Mrs. James Lawrence Breese. The amazingly well preserved garden is believed to be the work of Charles McKim; Stanford White, however, "is responsible for many of the garden details."[7] The garden still echoes the columned, porticoed house inspired by Mount Vernon. *House and Garden* magazine commented at the time: "One

might not have been surprised to have suddenly looked in upon it through some old Virginia hedge, but upon the wind-swept Long Island shore, its impression becomes doubly vivid…everything is green and white…"[8] Less than nine years earlier, Samuel Parrish commissioned landscape designer Warren Henry Manning (Manning had worked in the office of Frederick Law Olmstead, Sr. for eight years[9]) to create an arboretum on the grounds surrounding the Italianate museum he had built to house his collection of Renaissance paintings. After the building was completed, Parrish decided to commission for his gallery a sculpture series of copies of Roman emperors for which he asked the eminent sculptor Augustus Saint-Gaudens to select examples that were reproduced in Florence. The sculpture group was later removed to a courtyard outside.

Beginning in the Gilded Age and the first three decades of the twentieth century, many renowned gardens were established on the East End. While vast country estates elsewhere on Long Island dictated elaborate, European-inspired gardens, Hampton gardens were for the most part fairly conservative, usually larger and more formal in Southampton than farther east. Hampton gardens nurtured some of America's first professional women landscape architects, such as Marian Cruger Coffin, Annette Hoyt Flanders, Ellen Biddle Shipman, and Ruth Dean. Gardening and landscape design was considered then an art more "lady-like" than architecture and, therefore, a more "suitable" occupation for women. Ellen Shipman, who designed a significant garden in East Hampton, unequivocally said in a 1938 interview: "Until women took up landscaping, gardening in this country was at its lowest ebb. The renaissance of the art was due largely to the fact that women, instead of working over their boards, used plants as if they were painting pictures as an artist."[10]

When pioneer landscape architect Marian Cruger Coffin was commissioned to design Barberryland, a garden in the Shinnecock Hills near Southampton (1918–19) for Mr. and Mrs. Charles H. Sabin. She first persuaded her clients to buy a nearby farm and had the fertile topsoil removed to the "treeless plain" where she gradually turned it into a lush, flowering landscape. Coffin patiently planted an enclosed formal garden, a wild garden, and created winding flagstone paths leading to the bluff overlooking Peconic Bay.

Coffin designed five other gardens on the East End of Long Island, and in 1924 a childhood friend Henry Francis du Pont, who shared her passion for gardens and gardening, invited her to design the grounds of his Southampton summer home, Chestertown House. Again, the designer persuaded her client to purchase a farm in upstate New York and transport the topsoil to the dunes surrounding the site, where she planted a large assortment of native sea grasses and black pines.[11]

In nearby East Hampton, Louise Sheldon included in her book the garden Mrs. Lorenzo G. Woodhouse concocted in 1901 from a marsh behind her home. The garden became a source of inspiration for two American Impressionist artists, Childe Hassam and Gaines Ruger Donoho. Encompassing two acres, the painstakingly maintained garden contained a stream, pools and ponds, Japanese bridges, and two thatched teahouses. The garden was diagonally across Egypt Lane from where both artists lived and painted. The Cummings garden (as it was known after Mrs. Wood- house was widowed and remarried) is now part of the village nature trail. Another part of the property was donated by Donoho's widow in memory of the artist who had celebrated the accessible beauty of an extraordinary garden.

At The Creeks, a fifty-seven-acre tract of land overlooking Georgica Pond in East Hampton, two successive owners had created outstanding American gardens. Both were artists, both visionary gardeners, both as different as their times. The Creeks was a wedding gift to Albert and Adele Herter (from his

A somber assembly of copies of Roman portrait busts line an outdoor gallery in the arboretum de- signed by Warren Henry Manning, which surrounds the Italianate museum Samuel Parrish built to house his collection of Renaissance paintings in 1896.

parents), young artists who had met while studying in Paris. The couple camped out at various locations for months before choosing the perfect site for the Italianate house designed for them by architect Grosvenor Atterbury in 1899. Soon after the house was completed Adele Herter began designing a garden of almost an acre of radiating flowerbeds. For the entrance court, Herter planted a "garden of the sun" with yellow and orange flowers. On the pond side she planted a "garden of the moon" that contained blue and white flowers. Legend has it that thirty Japanese gardeners were brought in from overseas each summer to perform the endless task of weeding and watering.

Alfonso Ossorio saw The Creeks through very different eyes—those of a surrealist artist. In 1952, he bought The Creeks from the Herter's son Christian (Secretary of State during the Eisenhower administration) and imposed his highly personal vision on both the house and the gardens. (He painted the house black.) Ossorio gradually replanted the garden using many varieties of rare conifers as his primary medium, interspersed with his modernist polychrome sculptures, many made of found objects that became what the American Conifer Society has called "a living work of art."

Living well was the best revenge for Sara Wiborg Murphy, immortalized by F. Scott Fitzgerald as Nicole Diver in *Tender is the Night*. Sara's father, Frank Bestow Wiborg, "had bought a six-hundred-acre tract of ocean-front property"[12] west of the Maidstone Club in East Hampton. He then commissioned architect Grosvenor Atterbury to design a thirty-room summer home for his family in 1895 called The Dunes that overlooked a wide turf terrace and magnificent sunken garden filled with topiary trees and arching, rose-festooned arbors.

A renowned East Hampton garden that has been revived and restored is Gray Gardens. Looking back in *Forty Years of Gardening*, the garden autobiography she wrote in 1938, Anna Gilman Hill remembered the pleasure of sitting in the garden she had created: "You had a glimpse of blue water between dunes, high dunes, grass-covered and soft gray, like our walls… in this friendly place I realized my ideal."

To realize her ideal garden, Mrs. Hill set out in 1914 to transform the rough pasture of goldenrod and bayberry next to the ocean by erecting "cement walls high enough in some places to be pierced by arches with clanging wooden doors…arches recessed in the wall for seats and a fountain…a thatched tool house…an exedra [a leafy, shady recess] overlooking the sea." Mrs. Hill engaged a village carpenter and mason to fulfill her vision, filling her enclosed garden with flowers in pale colors and plants with gray foliage to complement "the soft gray dunes, cement walls, and sea mists."

In its next transformation, the garden was owned by John "Black Jack" Bouvier's sister and daughter (aunt and cousin of Jacqueline Bouvier Kennedy Onassis) who over the years gradually let Mrs. Hill's carefully tended garden return to an overgrown plot of briars, brambles, and bushes. Today the garden has been brought back to bloom by current owners Sally Quinn and Ben Bradlee.

Artist Robert Gwathmey had an in-house architect, his son. When twenty-seven-year-old Charles Gwathmey designed the elegantly spare, modernist house and studio in Amagansett for his parents in 1966, it not only changed the course of East End home design but American residential architecture as well.

Edward Albee succinctly says that his "natural" garden overlooking the edge of a bluff in Montauk "was designed by a hurricane." Albee placed a massive concrete and metal sculpture by Mia Westerlund-Roosen (1985) at the edge of the garden he has tended for more than forty summers.

Almost immediately, dunes and potato fields were sprouting with abstract expressions in architecture designed by the likes of Richard Meier, Paul Lester Weiner, and Gordon Bunshaft, all innovative and experimental in concept. Many of the new houses didn't have gardens and had little or no planting around them. The architects championed the theme of the relationship between the building and the natural beauty of the landscape. Landscape architect Ruth Dean, whose summer home overlooked Town Pond in East Hampton, was an early advocate of this notion. In her book *The Livable House, Its Garden* (published in 1917, it is one of the earliest landscape design books written by a female professional), she emphasized the harmonious relationship between house and garden. Dean was among the first landscape designers to encourage the use of indigenous trees and shrubs—a radical notion for gardeners who prized exotic foreign plants.

Ruth Dean emphatically explained that "a naturalistic [or a 'studied haphazard' as she sometimes dubbed it] garden calls for just as much planning as does a formal garden..."[13] More recently, Washington, D.C.–based Wolfgang Oehme and James van Sweden have designed many South Fork perennial gardens in their "new style" that creates a "natural" appearance.

After two decades of experimentation with the cutting-edge, architects began to look back at the shingles and cottages that have long been a distinguishing characteristic of Hampton homes. The postmodern house has stimulated a renewed interest in another cherished convention—gardens and gardening. The new gardens are as varied as the personalities of the people who design and develop them: some are rigidly formal, others harken back to traditional English cottage gardens. Oehme and van Sweden have also created "new style" gardens of whispering swathes of grasses interspersed with subtly colored foliage plants around postmodern houses.

The sun-washed landscape of the Hamptons, always flavored by the moist sea air and favored by a gentle climate that extends the growing season to encourage a vast variety of gardens that have flourished in its more than three-and-a-half-century history, is unique. As Mrs. Hill lovingly observed, "Gardening in Suffolk County spoils you for gardening in North America." □

Giverny transplanted: Beginning in the 1890s, the garden Claude Monet planned and planted at his home in Normandy has inspired generations of other artists and gardeners. In the East Hampton garden of William and Katharine Rayner, a flower-freckled turf path curving beneath metal arches mirrors Monet's masterpiece at Giverny.

PICTURING HAMPTON GARDENS

Plants are to the gardener what his palette is to a painter.[14]
—BEATRIX JONES FARRAND

MAN PLANTED A GARDEN before he built a house. In his effort to contain and nurture nature, he attempted to recreate the Paradise he lost. Gardening was at the beginning: civilization began to emerge when man could make sure of a plentiful provision of food by planting a garden.

A garden is an area of land enclosed for protection against outside invasion and the infestation of unwanted vegetation. The process of enclosure necessitated an arrangement within the confined space that led to organized order (design) in which to cultivate useful plants. By definition, this is a garden: a border of flowers or a plot of randomly placed plants is not!

The garden as the subject for a picture is comparatively recent in the history of art. Beatrix Jones Farrand, one of America's distinguished landscape architects, was born into a socially elite New York family portrayed in some of the novels of her aunt Edith Wharton. In an article Beatrix Joness wrote for *Scribner's* magazine in 1907, appropriately entitled *The*

Garden as a Picture, she succinctly stated: "The two arts of painting and garden design are closely related, except that the landscape gardener paints with actual color, line, and perspective to make a composition, as the maker of stained glass does, while the painter has but a flat surface on which to create his illusion: he has, however the incalculable advantage that no sane person would think of going behind a picture to see if it were equally interesting from that point of view."[15] Mrs. Farrand, who designed 22 gardens on Long Island, explained further that "a garden, large or small, must be treated in the Impressionist manner." This immediately brings to mind Mrs. Lorenzo G. Woodhouse's garden, painted by Childe Hassam and Gaines Ruger Donoho. Both American Impressionist artists chose for their subject almost identical views of their neighbor's nationally renowned water garden.

The artists had met in 1886 during the time they were students at the Académie Julian. Like so many other young American painters studying in Paris in the late 1880s, they were excited and influenced by the progressive trends of the French Impressionist painters.

Impressionism is best demonstrated in the paintings of Claude Monet, who had painstakingly planned and planted a sizeable garden at his home near Giverny, a Norman village some forty miles northwest of Paris. Monet's garden with its pond of floating water lilies crossed by a curving Japanese bridge became a massive still life of ever-changing colors and shapes that was the sole subject of his paintings throughout the final two decades of his life. Monet was one of the first artists to literally paint a portrait of a garden.

In 1891 Gaines Donoho bought a home and laid out a garden in East Hampton. Donoho's garden on Egypt Lane, like Monet's at Giverny, was one of his favorite painting places. Critic Royal Cortissoz wrote later: "He painted that garden over and over again in the same spirit in which he pottered over its flowers and hedges, loving it all…"[16]

Childe Hassam had been living and painting in New York City since his return from Europe in 1889. During the summer months the artist established a routine of leaving his city studio to paint in the coastal towns of New York and New England, including Cos Cob, Gloucester, and Appledore Island, one of the Isles of Shoals off the coast of New Hampshire. With the outbreak of the Spanish-American War in 1898, however, the island was deemed unsafe to visit because of its vulnerable location.

When Donoho learned that the artist's summer painting plans were disrupted by the war (they both lived in the same studio building at 130 West Fifty-Seventh Street), he urged his friend to come to East Hampton. After establishing himself and his wife Maude in one of the boarding houses of the village, Hassam began one of his first paintings of the region. The painting, *July Night*, evocatively depicts Maude at a lantern-lit Fourth of July party standing in the center of Donoho's garden. Hassam returned regularly to East Hampton, and in 1919 made the town his permanent summer residence when he bought Willow Bend, a house directly next to Donoho's property.

The first professionally trained artists to visit the East End of Long Island were a group of New York sketchers and painters who called themselves the Tile Club. Founded in 1877, the club members met to paint decorative tiles (then a popular art form) and exchange news and views about the New York art world. Founding members included Winslow Homer, John Twachtman, Edwin Austin Abbey, and J. Alden Weir. At their first annual dinner—held in Homer's Tenth Street studio—the "Tilers" planned a summer sketching expedition to the East End of Long Island. Homer, who spent several weeks painting in East Hampton in July 1874, most likely suggested the destination.

The Tilers arrived in East Hampton on the eleventh of June. They found comfortable lodgings at the Jonathan Baker farm on Further Lane and were soon outdoors, "bending assiduously over blocks and sketch books…" During that summer of 1878 the East End's future as a center of artistic enterprise was assured. Early the following year *Scribner's* magazine published the adventures of this "chirpy…hilarious group" in an article, "The Tile Club at Play." This enthusiastic account, illustrated with sketches made by club members of ocean vistas, bucolic landscapes, and blossom-filled gardens, intrigued fellow artists back home.

Tile Club members William Laffan and Edwin Austin Abbey vividly recounted to Thomas Moran and his artist-wife Mary Nimmo Moran the luminous light and old world atmosphere of East Hampton. Moran was nationally acclaimed as the "artist/explorer of the American West." As official artist, he had accompanied Dr. Ferdinand V. Hayden on his government-sponsored geological survey of the Yellowstone region in 1871. Moran's masterpiece was the first landscape painting included in the art collection of the United States Congress. Mary Nimmo Moran later became the first woman member of the New York Etching Club and the Royal Society of Painter-Etchers in London. Soon after visiting East Hampton, the Morans bought a sheep pasture across from Town Pond where, in 1884, they built an English Aesthetic Movement-inspired house that contained the first permanent, fully equipped artist's studio on the East End. The Moran house, thereafter called "The Studio," quickly became a gathering place for artists and townspeople alike. Thomas Wores painted the house and Mary Moran's garden bursting with blooms during a visit to East Hampton sometime between 1894 and 1900.

In Southampton, gardens had been planted and carefully cultivated since the settlement of the town in 1640. By the early 1870s and 1880s, artists such as Alfred C. Holland and Alfred Thompson Bricher, a mostly self-trained artist who is "best known for his shoreline scenes with breaking waves,"[17] began painting in Southampton. In 1881, Bricher married a local resident, Alice Robinson. On a sunny summer afternoon in 1883, he chose to portray the tranquil scene of his neighbor serenely sewing in her seashell-bordered garden.

Southampton became a Mecca for aspiring artists during the last decade of the nineteenth century when the premier American Impressionist painter, William Merritt Chase, established the Shinnecock Hills Summer School of Art at the invitation of local art enthusiasts (lead by Mrs. William Hoytt, Mrs. Henry Kirke Porter, and Samuel L. Parrish, who later built a museum to house his collection of art in Southampton). The school was the country's first for-

Teaching in the sun-bathed landscape near Southampton, William Merritt Chase took brush in hand to offer instruction by example to his students at the Shinnecock Hills Summer School of Art, about 1892.

mal open-air painting school and attracted a hundred or more students each season. Throughout the summer months, when Chase conducted classes, from 1891 to 1902 the windswept dunes, wave-washed beaches, and flower-filled gardens were punctuated with artists and easels.

A new generation of artists began arriving on the Eastern End of Long Island during and right after World War II. Fernand Léger and Lucia Wilcox spent a season in the East Hampton guest cottage of Sara (Wiborg) and Gerald Murphy. Max Ernst came with Peggy Guggenheim, and other surrealist artists soon followed, including André Breton and Marcel Duchamp. By the end of the war, the region had become an international center for artists; some stayed for a few months, others moved there permanently. In 1945 Jackson Pollock and Lee Krasner bought a modest farmhouse on Fireplace Road in The Springs section of East Hampton with a view of Accabonic

Harbor. Brooklyn-born Lee Krasner soon planted a garden beside the barn that Pollock had converted into a studio. As Ronald Pisano explained, "In The Springs, Pollock loved to putter around the house, visit with neighbors, and garden."[18] After Pollock's death in 1956, some recognizable imagery became apparent in Krasner's paintings which were inspired by the surrounding landscape, and perhaps, her garden.

Costantino Nivola, an accomplished artist in many media, and his wife Ruth bought a farmhouse with overgrown gardens just down the road from the Pollock property in 1948. After renovating the house, Nivola laid out and developed the garden with help from a friend, the Austrian architect Bernard Rudofsky. Nivola's garden became a series of open-air "rooms" creating an interplay of surfaces, sunshine, and succulent foliage that he used as an outdoor studio and gallery for his abstract sculpture and murals. Architectural historian Alastair Gordon speculates that Nivola

During the summer of 1953, Lee Krasner's neighbor Sam Duboff captured her in a 16mm home movie, cultivating the garden she had established beside her husband Jackson Pollock's studio on Fireplace Road in the Springs of East Hampton.

"may have made his most singular contribution to mid-century American culture in this garden."[19]

Not all artists had the patience to plan and "putter" in their garden. When Larry Rivers moved into his Southampton house and studio on Little Plains Road in 1951, he wanted an "instant garden." He painted life-size wooden cutouts of trees and shrubs and placed them in front of his studio creating a garden where the real coexisted with the surreal. Unfortunately, since Rivers' death in 2002, the artist's instant garden has disappeared.

"Gardening is like a painting never finished," says artist, gardener, and garden writer Robert Dash. For nearly forty years Dash has shaped, reshaped, and shaped again the garden in Sagaponack which he calls Madoo. Although the artist does not work directly from nature, he admits that the landscape and his nearly two-acre garden "has provided me with an almost reflex series of reactions—a vocabulary and a grammar"[20] for his art.

Almost a century ago many significant private Hampton gardens became the subject of the most modern means of picture making—photography. In the Teens and 1910s and '20s, talented commercial photographers (mostly women) journeyed out to the East End to take pictures of gardens for books, magazines, and periodicals, or for the garden owners themselves. These early garden photographs are unique documents of American landscape history, for today almost all the gardens have been altered or erased by neglect and time. Nothing is as it was at the beginning, but much of the appeal of Hampton gardens lies in the certainty that these beginnings have not been lost from sight. □

Some recognizable imagery became apparent in Lee Krasner's paintings in the late 1950s, such as *August Petals*, 1963, inspired by the landscape, and, perhaps the garden she planted and maintained in the Springs of East Hampton.

27

Opposite: Inspired by the paintings and illuminated pages found in medieval books of hours, Margaret Kerr's garden in the Springs of East Hampton contains many ingredients of a typical Hortus conclusus or enclosed garden with its centrally placed fountain surrounded by divided beds of fragrant herbs and other useful plants.

Top: Published in 1577 by Thomas Hyll, *The Gardener's Labyrinth* was one of the first Elizabethan books to offer instruction for cultivating a garden. A woodcut in the book depicts men working in a garden divided into raised rectilinear beds. Original settlers on the Eastern End of Long Island followed almost exactly the same gardening procedures.

Bottom: Directly behind the Southampton house built by Thomas Halsey in 1660 is a recreated garden that is a partial example of an early dooryard garden.

Opposite: Photographed in 1923, a bucolic view of the Mulford farm in East Hampton with the Pantigo Mill and Norman-style tower of Saint Luke's Church. At the end of the nineteenth century, American painters were captivated by the East End of Long Island with its centuries-old houses, windmills, and flower-filled gardens. East Hampton in particular seemed a town trapped in time.

Above: In back of the farmhouse acquired by Samuel Mulford in 1689 is a garden that simulated one planted by Rachel Mulford in 1780. Built in 1804 and moved to the property in 1917, the Pantigo Mill is one of the eleven surviving windmills that still charm visitors.

Opposite: A traditional bean tower or wigwam of cut saplings commands one of the raised beds surrounded by staked wooden planks in Rachel Mulfords's re-created dooryard garden. Plants in Rachel's garden supplied her family with "simples," or medicines, herbs for cooking, and dyes for coloring fabric.

Above: Close by the Mulford farm in East Hampton is another recreated dooryard garden at the side of the saltbox house John Howard Payne immortalized when he penned "Home, Sweet Home" in 1823. A pale or picket fence, whose principal function was to keep out animals, particularly rabbits, rodents, or marauding cows, encloses the garden. Both East Hampton gardens are open to the public.

On Shelter Island, the garden at Sylvester Manor has a continuous history of cultivation by the same family beginning in 1653. *Opposite:* The lower garden today still contains descendants of boxwood cuttings (*Buxus sempervirens,* now called American box) brought to America by Nathaniel Sylvester.

Above: A hand-colored glass lantern slide photograph (ca. 1905) of the enclosed garden at Sylvester Manor. Ancient boxwood almost obliterates the view of the second manor house, built in 1737. Lantern slides were made as teaching aids and for home entertainment beginning in the middle of the nineteenth century.

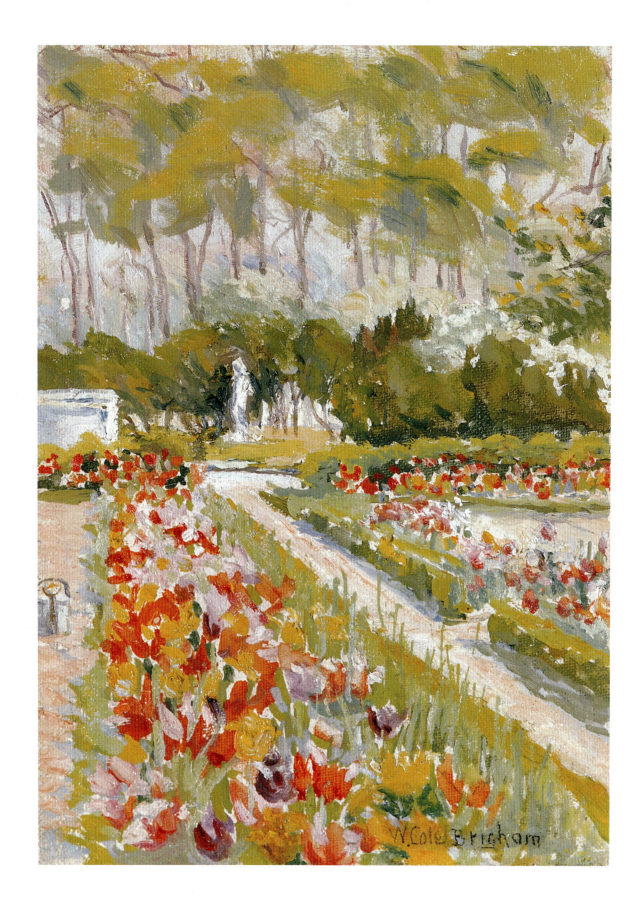

Opposite: Shelter Island artist Walter Cole Brigham painted *Tulip Beds, Sylvester Manor,* ca. 1920, in the colonial revival-style garden designed by Cornelia Horsford, the tenth proprietor of the manor, in the early spring. Both works depict the same garden.

Above: Wide stone steps lead into the elaborate sunken garden at Sylvester Manor in a turn-of-the-century hand-colored glass lantern slide.

Opposite top: The lower or sunken garden at Sylvester Manor, photographed by Frances Benjamin Johnston in 1900 for *Old Time Gardens* by Alice Morse Earl. *Opposite bottom:* Johnston photographed the garden staircase capped with finials leading into the sunken garden for *Beautiful Gardens in America* by Louise Shelton published in 1915.

Above: While visiting Cornelia Horsford, Mary Minna Morse, a New England artist, painted a watercolor of the garden with its towering ancient boxwood in *Garden Box, Sylvester Manor,* in 1895. The artist was a member of the prestigious Copley Society in Boston.

Alfred Thompson Bricher traveled out to Southampton in 1880 primarily to paint sea pictures. During the summer of 1883, he painted *In My Neighbor's Garden*, in which he depicted the tranquil scene of his neighbor sewing in her seashell-bordered garden with a distant view of Peconic Bay.

Opposite: Jessie Tarbox Beals framed her cumbersome box camera on the back porch of The Appletrees when she photographed the Southampton garden of Mr. and Mrs. Henry E. Coe for *Beautiful Gardens in America*, which Louise Shelton published in 1915.

Above: Crushed gravel paths and clipped boxwood borders surround the luxuriant midsummer garden filled with flowers at The Appletrees.

Captivated by the bucolic village and surrounding landscape of East Hampton, Thomas Moran and his artist-wife Mary Nimmo Moran built an English Aesthetic Movement–inspired house that contained the first artist's studio on the East End. Sometime between 1894 and 1900, Theodore Wores painted *Thomas Moran's House (top)* and *Thomas Moran's Garden (opposite),* bright with summer blossoms.
Top: Thomas Moran standing by the garden gate of The Studio, late 1890s.

Mary Nimmo married artist Thomas Moran in 1862. Although she painted, etching became a primary medium of expression that won her acclaim in both England and in America.

Opposite: Her sister-in-law Annette Parmentier Moran depicted her watering her garden at The Studio in *The Garden Walk (Mary Nimmo Moran Tending Her Garden)*, 1881.

Above: In 1895, Mary Moran painted her neighbor's garden in one of her few known works in oil, entitled *Dr. E. Osbourne's Garden*.

Opposite: The amazingly well-preserved Southampton garden behind the house designed for James Lawrence Breese by McKim, Mead, and White in 1906. The garden is thought to be designed by architect Charles McKim; Stanford White is responsible for the sculpture works and other details.

Above left: The original Doric pergola still surrounds three sides of the large formal garden. *Above right:* A marble sculpture group commissioned by Stanford White encircles part of the long, brick, herringbone-pattern walk that bisects the garden in a ca. 1920 photograph by Mattie Edwards Hewitt.

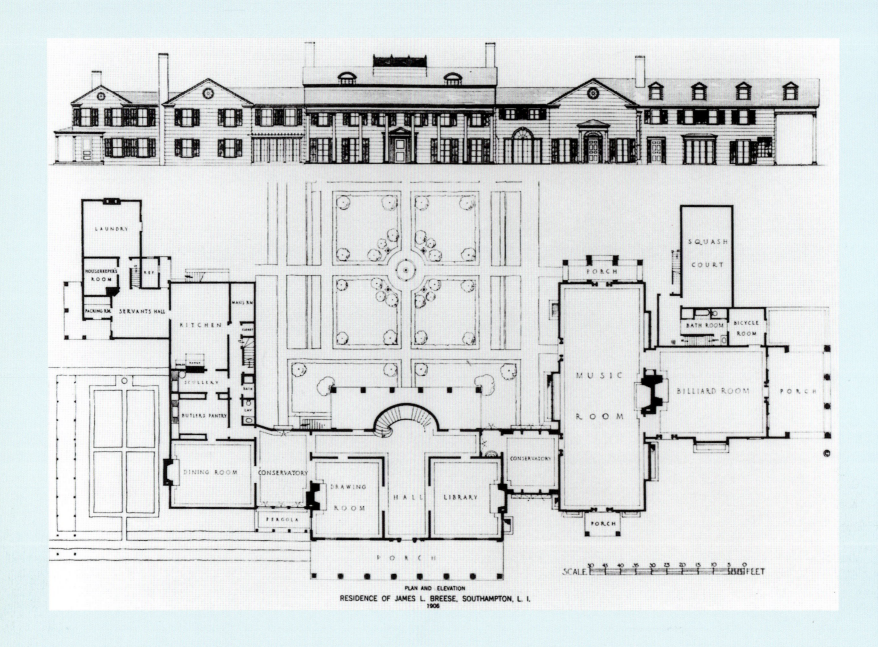

PLAN AND ELEVATION
RESIDENCE OF JAMES L. BREESE, SOUTHAMPTON, L. I.
1906

Above: The elevation and architectural plan for The Orchard included the formal garden that extended directly behind the house McKim, Mead, and White modeled after Mount Vernon.
Opposite top: Waving ornamental grasses surround the splashing fountain in the center of the garden.

Opposite bottom: Architect Stanford White commissioned and selected stone benches, urns, and sculpture for James Breese's garden in Southampton. Photographs by Miss Johnston-Mrs. Hewitt from *Beautiful Gardens in America*, 1915.

It was a homecoming, literally, when Walter Cole Brigham returned to Shelter Island early in 1899 to set up a studio overlooking Dering Harbor. Brigham had been studying at the Art Students League in New York and afterward spent a year painting in Florence. The artist painted two nearby views of *The Charles Lane Poor Gardens, Dering Harbor, Shelter Island, New York* in the late spring (*above*) and early summer (*opposite*) of 1935. Poor was a mayor of Dering Harbor and had large garden on his estate there.

When Mr. and Mrs. Charles H. Sabin commissioned pioneer landscape architect Marian Cruger Coffin to design their garden near Southampton (1918–1919), she persuaded them to buy a neighboring farm and transport the fertile topsoil to the wind-swept site in the Shinnecock Hills.

Opposite: The sunken garden at Barberryland with its semicircular lead fountain and pool.
Above: Enclosed on three sides, the lily pond and formal garden looks across Peconic Bay. Photographs by Mattie Edwards Hewitt, 1915.

Beginning in 1914, Henry Huddleston Rogers Jr. commissioned John Charles and his younger brother Frederick Law Olmsted, Jr., to design the extensive gardens and grounds of Black Point, his palatial home that faced south toward the sea in Southampton.

Opposite: Italian terracotta sculpture and urns accent the garden above a turf allée and lily pond.
Top: A view through an arching wall into the flower garden. Photographs by Samuel H. Gottscho, ca. 1920.
Bottom: Florence Vincent Robinson painted the watercolor of the *Lily Pond at Black Point* about 1919.

The garden Mrs. Lorenzo G. Woodhouse created in 1901 from a marsh behind her home on Huntting Lane in East Hampton was painted by Childe Hassam and Gaines Ruger Donoho. Both American Impressionist artists chose almost identical views of their neighbor's nationally renowned garden she called The Fens.

Opposite: Donoho painted *Woodhouse Water Garden* in the summer of 1911.
Above: Hassam painted *The [Woodhouse] Water Garden* adrift with Japanese sword-lilies (*Iris kaempferi*) in the early summer of 1909.

Above: Photographed about 1914, *Mrs. Stephen S. Cummins Water Garden* (as she was known after Mrs. Woodhouse was widowed and remarried) includes one of the two thatched Japanese tea houses in her garden at The Fens.

Above right: Photographed in 1925, a brick walk bordered by rows of clipped cones of rose of Sharon *(Hibiscus syriacus)*, August lilies *(Hosta Plantagineria)*, and drifts of astilbe leads to the entrance gate of The Fens on Hunnting Lane. The gateposts are still in place today.

Opposite: A leading member of the Peconic Art Colony, Caroline M. Bell painted Mrs. Woodhouse's East Hampton *Iris Garden* from inside the garden looking toward Hook Pond, ca. 1930.

Above: A hand-colored glass lantern slide of a photograph taken in 1915 by Miss Johnston-Mrs. Hewitt of an iris-bordered path leading to a thatched Japanese teahouse at The Fens.

In 1891, Gaines Ruger Donoho bought a house on Egypt Lane in East Hampton, where he established and maintained a garden that became a bottomless source of inspiration. He painted the box-bordered *Path to the Studio* about 1890–1900, which included the roof and central chimney of his neighbor Jonathan Baker's eighteenth-century shingled farmhouse.

Opposite: Landscape designer Marian Cruger Coffin enclosed a circular rose garden with a carefully shaped privet hedge at Crossways, the East Hampton home of Mr. and Mrs. William Wallace Benjamin.

Above: On nearby Jones Road, clipped boxwood cubes line a walk of brick squares leading to a pergola in the garden Ellen Biddle Shipman designed for the Misses Pruyn. Mattie Edwards Hewitt photographed it ca. 1925.

Opposite: When Albert and Adele Herter moved into the Italianate villa Grosvenor Atterbury designed for them in 1899, Adele Herter began planning a garden of almost an acre of flower beds radiating from a central fountain. Photograph, ca. 1925.

Above: A hand-colored glass lantern slide, ca. 1927, of the Herter's rambling East Hampton home, The Creeks, reflected in Georgica Pond that stretched almost to the ocean.

Opposite: On the pond side of The Creeks, Adele Herter planted a "garden of the moon" where she allowed only blue and white flowers to bloom. Graceful four- to five-foot spikes of Madonna lilies *(Lilium candidum)* illuminate and perfume the garden in mid-July. Autochrome by Frances Benjamin Johnston, 1927.

Above: Sweet alyssum *(Lobwlaria maritima)* borders a turf path curving toward the east side of the house at The Creeks. Photographed by Frances Benjamin Johnston in 1915.

THE CREEKS: OSSORIO

Surrealist artist Alfonso Ossorio bought The Creeks in 1952 and eventually completely resculpted the garden that the Herters planted in 1899 with his highly personal vision. Linda Alpern photographed a kaleidoscopic tapestry of rare conifers interspersed with indigenous trees and shrubs in October 1989.

Alfonso Ossorio planted the almost sixty-acre garden at The Creeks in East Hampton with his collection of rare conifers interspersed with his modernist polychrome sculptures, many made of found objects that became what the American Conifer Society called "a living work of art." Ossorio designed and photographed his new-wave swimming pool in 1989.

Above: During the winter of 1990, Linda Alpert photographed The Creeks sculpted by snow.

Above: The splendid sunken garden filled with topiary trees and arching, rose-festooned arbors at The Dunes, the Frank B. Wiborg mansion in East Hampton was acclaimed in a hand-colored post card, ca. 1920.

Opposite top: Mattie Edwards Hewitt photographed the vast garden at The Dunes with a view overlooking Hook Pond, ca. 1924.

Opposite bottom: Frances Benjamin Johnston's hand-colored glass lantern slide photograph depicted a circular pond in the garden surrounded by rose-covered walls in June, ca. 1920s.

Mr. and Mrs. Robert C. Hill bought a twenty-eight-room "summer cottage" at the western end of Lily Pond Lane in East Hampton in 1913. Anna Gilman Hill, a dedicated gardener and garden writer, built a walled garden to temper the sea winds and salt spray. "It was a truly gray garden" she wrote later, "only low gray-foliaged plants such as neptha, stachys, and pinks...were allowed inside the walls..."

Above: Frances Benjamin Johnston photographed the garden enclosed by "cement walls high enough in some places to be pierced by arches with clanging wooden doors—a thatched tool shed—an exedra overlooking the sea," ca. 1920.
Opposite: A hand-colored glass lantern slide of Mrs. Hill's Gray Garden filled with summer blossoms, ca. 1925.

Left: Gray Gardens has been brought back to bloom today by Sally Quinn and Ben Bradlee with the help of garden designer Victoria Fensterer, who added Betty Prior roses, mimosa trees, and peegee hydrangeas. *Above:* Mattie Edwards Hewitt photographed Mrs. Hill's enclosed garden "pierced by arches with clanging wooden doors" and the thatched tool house in 1923.

Looking back in *Forty Years of Gardening*, an autobiography Mrs. Hill published in 1938, she remembered the pleasures of sitting in the exedra at the end of the garden: "You had a glimpse of blue water between dunes—high dunes, grass-covered and soft gray, like our walls..."

Opposite: Mattie Edwards Hewitt photographed Mrs. Hill's exedra and enclosed Gray Gardens in 1923.
Above: Mrs. Hill's rose-encrusted exedra on a perfect afternoon in June.

83

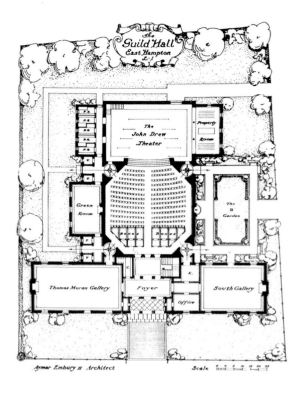

Architect Amar Embury II designed the East Hampton Free Library in 1911, and, in 1931, the Guild Hall across the street. His wife, landscape architect Ruth Dean, designed the gardens for both institutions.

Opposite bottom: Soon after the dedication of the Guild Hall on August 19, 1931, Childe Hassam made an etching of the entrance of the building that shows newly-planted shrubbery by Dean.

Opposite top left: Entrance to the side garden of Guild Hall designed by Dean.

Opposite top right: Embury's original architectural plan for Guild Hall included landscaping by Dean.

Top: After Dean's untimely death in 1932, Embury designed and placed a fountain in her memory in the wall of the garden she designed at Guild Hall.

Above: One of Dean's favorite shrubs, a Rose Bay (*rhododendron maximum*)—the largest native species of rhododendron—was photographed flourishing in July of 1924 by Samuel H. Gottscho in the "naturalistic" garden designed by Dean, located directly behind the East Hampton Library.

Extending from Lily Pond Lane in East Hampton to the ocean, the garden preserved and improved by Donald and Polly Bruckmann encompasses almost seven acres of seaside and dune gardens, a pond surrounded by native woodland plants, and a formal rose garden.

Opposite: Spangled with new growth, a yew hedge surrounds an ancient carved wellhead overflowing with foaming verbena plants.

Above: Designed by Grosvener Atterbury in 1916, the Bruckmann house overlooks the pond and "natural" garden of native trees and plants. Donald Bruckmann, a former Chairman of the Board of Managers of the New York Botanical Garden, was an early advocate of banning insecticides in his garden.

Designed and planted in 1912, the extensive garden behind Coxwould on Lily Pond Lane in East Hampton had deteriorated into a nondescript backyard until its new owners Lowell Schulman and Dianne Wallace commissioned landscape designer Edwina van Gal to revive the neglected space. Van Gal created a series of thirteen connecting "rooms" in the garden that can be viewed from the windows and wide terrace stretching behind the house.

Opposite: Enclosed by a high privet *(Ligustrum vulgare)*, van Gal created an all-green parterre garden of boxwood *(Buxus sempervirens)* punctuated with terracotta tubs of sphere-shaped yew trees.
Above: In the cutting garden at Coxwould a stone sundial records only the brightest summer hours.

Designer Charlotte Moss, who creates luxurious interiors, worked on the exterior of her East Hampton home with landscape architect Lisa Stamm and her architect husband-partner Dale Booher.
Above left: Broad-leafed plantain lilies *(Hosta sieboldiana)* border a curving path leading to a stone obelisk with potted tropical sago palms around the base.

Above right: Graceful stone steps adorned by Victorian urns lead to the lower garden at Boxwood Terrace.
Opposite: The potagerie, as Moss calls her vegetable and cutting garden, boasts tall topiary bay trees bordered by clipped box *(Buxus "Justin Brouwers").*

Opposite: When he was asked to create a natural woodland garden for a client in Water Mill, landscape designer Jack Whitmore traveled to the mountains of Pennsylvania to select rocks and stones and transported them to the site along with mature specimen trees and other varieties of plant material.

Above: Snow softens the black winter-bones of the garden with its waterfall gently flowing into a placid pond.

93

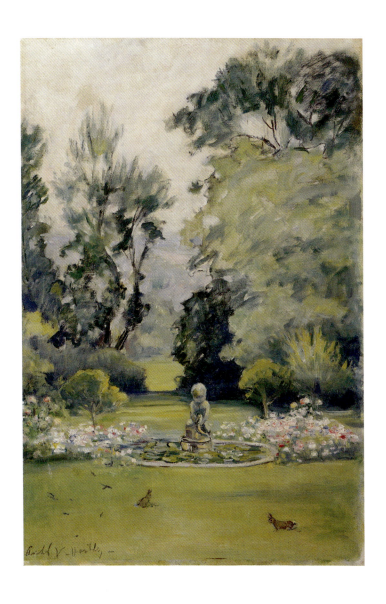

All in the family: Rachel Hartley's grandfather was Hudson River School painter, George Inness. Her father Jonathan Scott Hartley sculpted the figure for the garden behind their home in the Hampton Park district of Southampton. Rachel Hartley painted *Winter Garden in Southampton (opposite)*, shrouded in snow, and transformed in *Summer Garden in Southampton (above)*. Both paintings are ca. 1930.

Walking through the garden at Woody House, William and Katharine Rayner's home that sits twenty feet above a bluff overlooking both the ocean and Georgica Pond, a visitor encounters a series of ever-changing vistas designed by Ryan Gainey that combine to create a complete garden experience.

Opposite: An arching pergola stretches above the Mediterranean walk where in midsummer the many shades of purple shrubs and plants predominate.

Above left: Lotus and papyrus are reflected in a narrow canal in the Mogul Garden fed by an elephant fountain of carved stone.

Above right: Fiery wands of *"Lucifer"* lilies blaze in another part of the garden inspired by Persian and northern Indian garden designs.

Laid out geometrically, the cutting garden at Woody House contains a dramatic dome composed of four espaliered pears (*Pyrus celleryana*) that is enclosed by a Belgian fence of apple trees. Beds in the garden are planted with annuals, perennials, and vegetables ready for cutting and picking throughout the growing season. *Opposite*: Peering across the garden toward Georgica Pond is artist William Rayner's light-washed studio tower. *Above*: A board-banded bed in the cutting garden is surrounded by terracotta paving tiles.

Annuals and perennials provide a patchwork of brilliant color throughout the summer months in the Water Mill garden of Neil Hirsch. Landscape designer Jack Whitmore surrounded the bright beds with waist-high hedges of purple barberry *(Berberis thumbergii)*. The manicured lawn gently slopes to the edge of Mecox Bay.

Opposite: Costantino Nivola sculpted a metal fountain that contributes another dimension to his garden in the Springs of East Hampton—that of sound. Behind the splashing fountain, the sculptor erected a concrete wall where, before it set, he inscribed a frieze of allegorical figures basking in the sun.

Above: Halfway between his house and studio, Nivola arranged three large luscious fruits he carved from concrete; over the years they have been embellished with lichens and moss. Vintage photograph courtesy of Ruth Nivola, ca. 1955.

COSTANTINO NIVOLA

Costantino Nivola designed a geometric colonade for his garden in The Springs that echoes shade-providing structures he remembered from Orani, his hometown in central Sardinia. The artist began creating the garden soon after he bought a neglected farmhouse and thirty-five-acre piece of property not far from downtown East Hampton, in 1948.

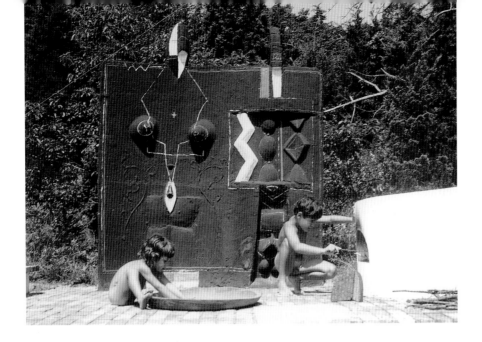

Opposite: Trained as a mason, Nivola used his garden as an outdoor studio and sculpture gallery where one large work has become entwined by an aggressive native trumpet creeper *(Campsis radicans)* that in midsummer crowns the sculpture with reddish-orange blooms.
Top: The two Nivola children, Claire and Pietro, playing in front of one of their father's massive painted cement sculptures.
Bottom: Etched by snow, a mural-enhanced solarium the sculptor built for secluded sunbathing. Vintage photographs courtesy of Ruth Nivola, ca. 1955.

For nearly forty years, artist, gardener, and garden writer Robert Dash has shaped, rethought, and shaped again his garden in Sagaponack. He calls his house Madoo, and its garden sprawls over nearly two acres not far from the ocean.

Opposite: A gleaming arch defines a box-edged path leading to the guesthouse.

Above: "The art of the garden and the art of the studio have separate identities" declares Dash, "but each nourishes the other." Like many other of his paintings, *New Weather (1983)* represents many gardens, whereas Madoo, the garden, is a painterly composition of constantly changing colors, form, and light.

Garden geometry: *Above:* At Madoo, Robert Dash designed a parterre garden of intertwined clipped box *(Buxus vardar valley)* and *(Buxus suffriticosa)* that hearkens back to seventeenth-century "knot" or "knott" gardens of England and Europe. Later, in the eighteenth century, knots became popular in gardens of the gentry along the eastern sea-board. A visitor to Washington's garden at Mount Vernon in 1779 described it as: "Very handsomely laid out in squares and flower knots..."

Opposite: In another part of the garden, Dash contrived a living "instillation" of *Ginko biloba* trees interspersed with spheres of clipped box *(Buxus suffriticosa)*. Chemicals are not allowed in the garden at Madoo; visitors are. The garden is open to the public.

In Bridgehampton, Cornelia Foss finds inspiration for her paintings close by: landscapes, seascapes, and the garden she plants and tends just outside her home and studio. "When I think of Eastern Long Island and its long history of painters who have wondered its fields and dunes, I am always reminded of my favorite quotation from Cézanne: 'the same subject for study seen from different angles gives a subject for study... I think I could be occupied for months without changing my place, simply bending a little more to the right or left.'"[21]

Opposite: The artist's lush dooryard garden in midsummer. *Above:* Foss's Summer Garden, painted in 2003.

Landscape historian Leslie Rose Close's Bridgehampton garden is a startling mix of herb, vegetable, and ornamental plants.

Opposite: Hollyhocks, sunflowers *(Helianthus annus)*, and Verbascum *(V. olympicum)* tower above the wooden walk to the studio of her husband, artist Chuck Close.

Above: A row of exotic Egyptian onions flourish in another part of the garden.

Below: Sage *(Salvia offficinalis),* angelica *(A. archangelica),* Siberian iris *(Iris sibirica),* and a Dutchman's pipe vine *(Aristolochia durior)* climbs the edge of the studio in early June. Photographs by Linda Alpern, 2003.

Opposite: Curving above the entrance gate to his newly acquired "Park," as Donald Sultan calls it, stands a towering rose of Sharon *(Hibiscus syriacus)*, a shrub radiant with midsummer blooms. The weathered gate and fence have been in place since the nineteenth century next to the artist's 1660 house in Sag Harbor.

Above: Morning Glories, July 1988, are among the recognizable plant imagery in Sultan's paintings and prints, simultaneously representational and abstract. Over the years, fruit, flowers, and plant material have been a source of inspiration for paintings and prints.

Textile designer, collector, and gardener Jack Lenor Larsen assembled long, low berms of soil and sand, and established lawns and defined spaces as background settings for his plant and sculpture collections in the Northwest Woods of East Hampton.

Opposite: Standing Figure by Margaret Israel overlooks the lap pool bordered by high clipped hedges.

Above left: One of the twenty-two-foot-tall columns that define the open-air summer living room at LongHouse.

Above right: Two of Grace Knowlton's twelve copper forms, *Untitled*, anchor the lawn near Peter's Pond.

Opposite: In the summer of 2003, Peter's Pond at LongHouse inspired the painting *Pond at Long-House* by Ty Stroudsburg. The fifteen-acre garden and arboretum that is open to the public draws about seven thousand visitors annually.

Above: Textile designer Jack Lenor Larsen began creating a garden for sculpture at LongHouse just outside of East Hampton more than fifteen years ago. *Cobalt Reeds* by glass-blowing wizard Dale Chihuly pierce the edge of the lotus-filled pond.

Conifers, flowering trees and shrubs, bamboo, ornamental grasses, day lilies, and other perennials provide four-season delights for visitors to LongHouse. *Opposite:* Safety pins are the principal medium for *August Grove*, a sculpture group created by Tamiko Kawata that Larsen placed in a rushing stream of sand.

Top: At the edge of a sloping berm, identical corten steel boxes are the focus in one of the gardens of the fifteen-acre landscape preserve outside of East Hampton. *Bottom:* The garden as an art form is clearly exemplified in an installation Ron Rudnicki calls *Angles of Repose*.

Above: Just outside of East Hampton, Jack Lenor Larsen's fifteen-acre garden is studded with more than forty sculptures he strategically placed around the grounds and pond. "So much work looks best in gardens as foliage provides a superb texture for contrast," Larsen explains. *August Grove,* a sculpture installation by Tamiko Kawata, is the focal point of a sweeping sand berm dissolving into the "natural" background in one area of the garden.

Opposite: Textile designer, collector, and gardener Jack Lenor Larsen installed a double row of painted cedar posts he calls "Study in Heightened Perspective" in his garden in the Northwest Woods of East Hampton.

Rocks have always been the significant element in Chinese and Japanese gardens. For centuries their shape, color, and texture were admired and praised in both countries.

Opposite: Masses of mammoth imported rocks were the material of choice when Jack Whitmore designed the distinctive garden at the Moreton Binn estate on Further Lane in Amagansett.

Above: Myriad shapes and subtle shadings of rocks and stones have been an obsession and inspiration for Robert Richenburg, a second-generation Abstract Expressionist who has been collecting, arranging, and rearranging his rock garden in The Springs of East Hampton.

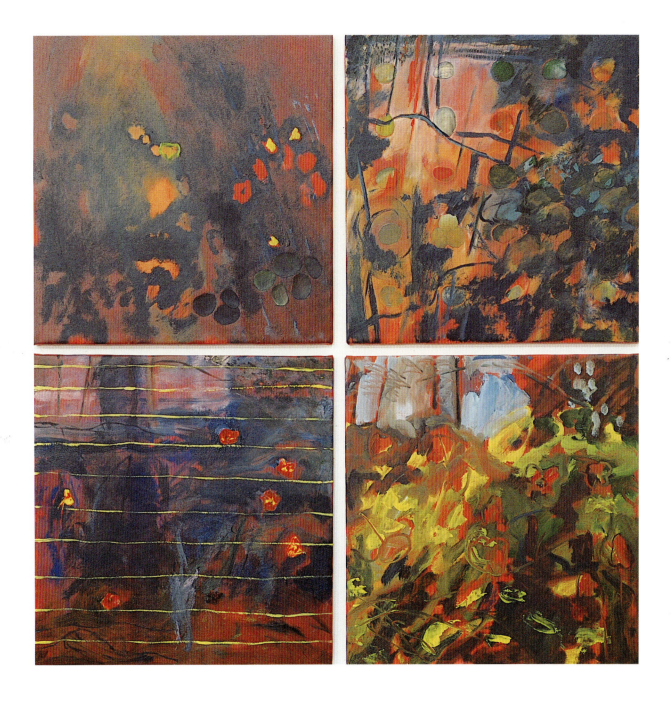

"What's more abstract than a garden?" theorizes avid gardener and artist Roy Nicholson, whose paintings skirt the slim edge between representation and abstraction.

Opposite: Nicholson erected a square arbor of cedar saplings to support scarlet runner-beans which give symmetry, scale, and perspective to his Sag Harbor garden aglow with indigenous black-eyed Susans *(Rudibeckia hirta)* and towering Joe-Pye weed *(Eupatorium purpureum).*

Above: Gloaming Group # 5 (2001) incorporates many natural images derived from the artist's garden.

At the time landscape designer and author Lois Sherr began to recast the parking court in front of her sister's East Hampton house into an outdoor garden room, the color purple, her sister Lynn Sherr's favorite color, became the obvious choice.

Opposite: Borders brimming with purple annual and perennial plants in the four-season garden surrounded on one side by a "wall" of purple-leaf plum trees. *Above:* Muted red Sedona stone cover the edges of the quadrangular lily pool and pavement that extends to the contemporary house.

Opposite top: A wide crushed gravel walk is bordered by a hedge of clipped yew and banks of rhododendron (Roseum elegans) bisecting part of Gerson Leiber's almost-green garden in the Springs of East Hampton.
Opposite bottom: Soaring juniper (Juuniperus chinensis) trees and an "eye-catching" stone obelisk punctuate his garden that Leiber says "is distinguished by hedges, and trellises which I had built, which are also geometric shapes."[22]
Above: Lightless Garden (2002) is one of many neocubist paintings inspired by the garden Leiber designed and planted almost half a century ago.

Opposite: Swirling branches of weeping willow *(Salix babylonica)* frame the view of a collect pond or "scuttle" hole created by the Wisconsin Glacier some twenty-five thousand years ago in the "natural" garden behind the Shelter Island home of husband and wife landscape design team Dale Booher and Lisa Stamm. Booher designed the pier and red bench that visually anchors the pond. *Above:* Russian olive and black pine trees silhouette the perspective from the edge of Jennifer Bartlett's Amagansett as it blends into the "natural" landscape behind her house and studio in the pastel, *October, Amagansett # 11* (MM).

Opposite: Swaths of swaying grasses and foliage plants create abstract patterns through all seasons in the Water Mill garden that landscape designers Wolfgang Oehme and James van Sweden created for Carole and Alex Rosenberg.

Above: Masses of flowering ghost weed *(Euphorbia palustris)* are among the more than one hundred trees, shrubs, ornamental grasses, sedges, rushes, and bamboo that the Washington, D.C.-based landscape team planted to provide a great variety of textural contrast in the garden.

Opposite: Oehme and van Sweden meticulously planned the Water Mill garden to create a natural appearance that blends into the landscape at the edge of Mecox Bay and beyond.
Above: Looking out of her airy studio near Water Mill in 1994, Jane Freilicher painted *Beginning of Summer*.

Known for the ever-changing views she paints from her studio windows, the artist included milkweed (*Asclepias syriack*) and Rosa rugosa thriving at the edge of her natural garden where a curving path leads through clumps of black pines to Mecox Bay.

"A place means a lot to me..." Fairfield Porter once explained. Southampton was such a place. Porter spent more than a quarter-century there, painting its seascapes and landscapes. Looking outside of his Main Street home one spring morning in 1960, the artist portrayed *Backyards at Southampton*, including some of his near neighbors' gardens.

NOTES

1 Leslie Rose Close, "Alfonso Ossorio's Garden at The Creeks," *East Hampton Star*, April 9, 1988, p. IV–3.

2 Ruth Dean, *The Livable House, Its Garden* (New York: Moffatt Yard & Company, 1917).

3 John A. Strong, *The Algonquian Peoples of Long Island: From Earliest Times to 1700* (Interlaken, New York: Empire State Books, 1997), p. 95.

4 Ibid., p. 100.

5 U. P. Hedrick, *A History of Horticulture in America: To 1860* (Portland, Oregon: Timber Press, 1950, reprint 1988), p. 26.

6 Cornelia Horsford, "The Manor House of Shelter Island," an address read before the annual meeting of The Order of Colonial Lords of Manors in America on April 23, 1931 (New York: printed privately, 1934).

7 MacKay, Baker, and Traynor, *Long Island Country Houses and Their Architects, 1860–1940*, (New York: Society of the Preservation of Long Island Antiquities and W.W. Norton, 1997), p. 117.

8 *House & Garden*, March 1903, p. 117–126.

9 Charles A. Birnbaum, Robin Karson, et al., *Pioneers of American Landscape Design* (New York: National Park Service of Landscape Initiative, Library of American Landscape History, Catalogue of Landscape Records in the United States at Wave Hill, Cultural Landscape Foundation and McGraw-Hill, 2000), p. 236.

10 Ibid., p. 346.

11 MacKay, Baker, and Traynor, *Long Island Country Houses and Their Architects, 1860–1940*, p. 117.

12 Calvin Tompkins, *Living Well is the Best Revenge*, (New York: The Viking Press, 1962), p. 17.

13 Ruth Dean, *The Livable House, Its Garden*.

14 Beatrix Jones [Farrand], "The Garden as a Picture," *Scribner's* magazine, 1917, p. 2.

15 Ibid., p.2.

16 Royal Cortissoz, "An Artist Made Better Known Since His Death," *New York Tribune*, November, 1916.

17 Ronald G. Pisano, *Long Island Landscape Painting 1820–1920*, (Boston: New York Graphic Society, 1985), p. 54.

18 Ronald G. Pisano, *Long Island Landscape Painting Volume II, The Twentieth Century* (Boston: Bulfinch Press, 1990), p.80.

19 Alastair Gordon, "A Garden Vestige of the Paint-Splattered Hamptons," *The New York Times*, March 1, 2001, p. F7.

20 Ronald G. Pisano, *Long Island Landscape Painting Volume II: The Twentieth Century*, p. 102.

21 Dore Ashton, *Cornelia Foss, 2001*, exhibition catalogue, New York City: DFN Gallery, 2001, p. 2.

22 Gerrit Henry, *Gerson Leiber: "My Garden,"* exhibition catalogue, New York City: Denise Bibor Fine Art, Inc., 2001, p. 3.

23 Helen Harrison, *Nicolai Cikovsky*, exhibition catalogue, Southampton, New York: Parrish Art Museum, 1980.

An architect turned artist, Allen Townsend Terrell painted an East End garden bursting with *Summer Flowers* (1927) illuminated by scarlet splashes of salvia (*S. splendens*) and zinnia (*Z. elegans*).

Unlike most artists, the landscape of eastern Long Island came as no surprise to Sheridan Lord, who had spent the idyllic summers of his childhood there. Surprising or not, the artist spent the most productive years of his life in a house in the middle of a potato field in Sagaponack. It took Lord four successive Aprils, working two or three weeks each year, to complete *Landscape, April 1988-89-90-91*, a painting of his wife's working garden at the back of their property in Sagaponack. His wife Pamela is a landscape designer and writer.

BIBLIOGRAPHY

Brown, Jane. *Beatrix: the Gardening Life of Beatrix Jones Farrand, 1872–1959*. New York: Viking, 1995.

Birnbaum, Charles A.; Karson, Robin, et al. *Pioneers of American Landscape Design*. New York: National Park Service of Landscape Initiative, Library of American Landscape History, Catalogue of Landscape Records in the United States at Wave Hill, Cultural Landscape Foundation and McGraw-Hill, 2000.

Cameron, Katharine. *The Moran Family Legacy*. East Hampton, New York: Guild Hall Museum, 1998.

Canaday, John. *Mainstreams of Modern Art*. New York: Simon & Schuster, 1959.

Close, Leslie Rose. *Portrait of an Era in Landscape Architecture: The Photographs of Mattie Edwards Hewitt*. Bronx, New York: Wave Hill, 1983.

Close, Leslie Rose. "Alfonso Ossorio's Garden at The Creeks," *The East Hampton Star*, April 9, 1998.

Cortissoz, Royal. "An Artist Better Known Since His Death," *New York Tribune*, November, 1916.

Dean, Ruth. *The Livable House; Its Garden*. New York: Moffat Yard & Company, 1917.

Earl, Alice Morse. *Old Time Gardens*. New York: The Macmillan Company, 1901.

Eberlein, Harold Donilson. *Manor Houses and Historic Homes of Long Island and Staten Island*. New York: J.B. Lippincott, Co., 1928.

Epstein, Jason, and Elizabeth Barlow. *East Hampton: A History and Guide*. New York: Random House, 1985.

Esten, Gilbert, Wood. *Hampton Style*. Boston: Little, Brown and Company, 1993.

Esten, John. *Childe Hassam: East Hampton Summers*. East Hampton, New York: Guild Hall Museum, 1997.

Fleming, Nancy. *Money, Manure & Maintenance: Ingredients for Successful Gardens of Marian Coffin, 1876–1957*. Weston, Massachusetts: Country Place Books, 1995.

Fort, Ilene Susan. *Childe Hassam's New York*. San Francisco, California: Pomegranate Artbooks, 1993.

Gordon, Alastair. "A Garden Vestige of the Paint-Splattered Hamptons," *The New York Times*, March 1, 2001.

Gordon, Robert, and Sydney Eddison, *Monet the Gardner*. New York: Universe, 2002.

Griswold, Mac, and Eleanor Weller. *Golden Age of American Gardens: Proud Owners, Private Estates*. New York: Harry N. Abrams, 1991.

Hefner, Robert J., ed. *East Hampton's Heritage: An Illustrated Architectural Record*. New York: W.W. Norton & Company, 1982.

Hill, Anna Gilman. *Forty Years of Gardening.* New York: Frederick A. Stokes Company, 1938.

Hobhouse, Penelope. *Gardening Through the Ages.* New York: Simon & Schuster, 1992.

Horsford, Cornelia. "The Manor of Shelter Island." Printed privately, 1934.

Landau, Ellen G. *Lee Krasner: A Catalogue Raisonné.* New York: Harry N. Abrams, 1995.

Leighton, Ann. *American Gardens in the Eighteenth Century.* Boston: Houghton Mifflin Company, 1976.

Leighton, Ann. *Early American Gardens.* Boston: Houghton Mifflin Company, 1970.

Lockwood, Alice T. *Gardens of Colony and State.* New York: Charles Scribner's Sons, 1931.

The Long Island Country House 1870–1930. The Parrish Art Museum. Los Angeles: Perpetua Press, 1988.

Ludman, Joan. *Fairfield Porter: A Catalogue Raisonné.* New York: Hudson Hills Press, 2001.

MacKay, Baker and Traynor. *Long Island Country Houses and Their Architects, 1860–1940.* New York: Society of the Preservation of Long Island Antiquities and W.W. Norton & Company, 1997.

Pisano, Ronald G. *Long Island Landscape Painting, 1820–1920.* Boston: New York Graphic Society, 1988.

Pisano, Ronald G. *Long Island Landscape Painting, Vol. II, The Twentieth Century.* Boston: Bulfinch Press, 1990.

Punch, Walter T., gen. ed. *A History of Gardening in America.* Massachusetts Horticultural Society. Boston: Bulfinch Press, 1992.

Rae, John W. *Images of America: East Hampton.* Charleston, South Carolina: Arcadia Publishing, 2001.

Rose, Barbara. *Krasner/Pollock: A Working Relationship.* East Hampton, New York: Guild Hall Museum, 1981.

Shelton, Louise. *Beautiful Gardens in America.* New York: Charles Scribner's Sons, 1914 (revised 1924).

Southgate, Patsy. "Lavish Legacy," *The East Hampton Star,* March 25, 1989.

Thomas, William, et al. *Whitmore's Private Hampton Gardens.* Harper, Miller & Co., East Hampton, New York, 2001.

Tompkins, Calvin. *Living Well is the Best Revenge.* New York: The Viking Press, 1962.

Van der Donck, Adrian. *A Description of the New-Netherlands.* Amsterdam, 1655.

Wilson, Thurman. *Thomas Moran, Artist of the Mountain.* Norman: University of Oklahoma Press, 1966.

Mattie Edwards Hewitt photographed the completely enclosed Southampton garden of Mr. and Mrs. G. Warrington Curtis resplendent with spikes of hollyhocks (*Althea rosea*) during the midsummer of 1914.

RAE FERREN

Parochial pride: "By the time the wisteria does the right thing by framing a neat East Hampton doorway, yes, just like a picture postcard—I'll head for home in The Springs and marvel at the oaks and cedars on one violet blues," says Rae Ferren. *The Flowering,* painted in 1993, is one the artist's many works inspired by the light-blessed East End landscape and gardens where she has lived for more than thirty years.

LIST OF ILLUSTRATIONS

Numbers refer to pages on which illustrations appear. Height precedes width. All new four-color photographs by Evelene Wechsler are not noted.

ENDPAPERS: Garden plan of Neil Hirsch estate in Water Mill, New York, by Jack Whitmore, East Hampton, New York.

2. Walter Cole Brigham (1870–1941), *Up the Brick Walk, Late Afternoon*, ca. 1935. Oil on canvasboard, 7 x 5 inches. Wallace Gallery, East Hampton, New York.

5. *The Creeks*, East Hampton, New York, November, 1990. Photograph by Linda Alpern.

11. Leo Revi 1943–), *July Garden, The Circle*, 1976. Oil on linen, 30 x 24 inches. Hampton Roads Gallery, Southampton, New York.

12. Childe Hassam (1859–1935), *Old House and Garden, East Hampton, Long Island,* 1898. Oil on canvas, 24$\frac{1}{16}$ x 20 inches. Henry Art Gallery, University of Washington, Seattle, Horace C. Henry Collection.

23. William Merritt Chase outdoors demonstrating before the Shinnecock Summer School of Art Class, ca. 1892. Albumen print, 4$\frac{3}{4}$ x 6$\frac{3}{8}$ inches. William Merritt Chase Archives, Parrish Art Museum, Southampton, New York. Gift of Jackson Chase Storm.

24. Sam Duboff, *Lee Krasner in Her Flower Garden, East Hampton,* 1953. Still image from a 16mm home movie. Pollock-Krasner House and Study Center, East Hampton, New York.

27. Lee Krasner (1908–1984), *August Petals*, 1963. Oil on canvas, 55 x 48 inches. Robert Miller Gallery, New York City.

29. Thomas Hyll, *The Gardener's Labyrinth*, 1577. Woodcut.

30. Eugene Armbruster, *Mulford Farm*, 1923. Albumen print, 4 x 3$\frac{1}{8}$ inches. New York Public Library, Special Collections.

35. *Sylvester Manor, Shelter Island, New York*, ca. 1915. Hand-colored glass lantern slide photograph. Archives of American Gardens, Garden Club of America Collection, Smithsonian Institution, Washington, D.C.

36. Walter Cole Brigham, *Tulip Beds at Sylvester Manor*, ca. 1920. Oil on panel, 7 x 5 inches. Wallace Gallery, East Hampton, New York.

37. *Sylvester Manor, Shelter Island, New York*, ca. 1915. Hand-colored glass lantern slide photograph. Archives of American Gardens, Garden Club of America Collection, Smithsonian Institution, Washington, D.C.

38. Frances Benjamin Johnston, *Lower Garden, Sylvester Manor*, 1900. Photograph in *Old Time Gardens* by Alice Morse Earl.

Frances Benjamin Johnston, *Lower Garden, Sylvester Manor*, 1915. Photograph in *Beautiful Gardens of America* by Louise Shelton.

39. Mary Minna Morse (1859–?), *Garden Box, Sylvester Manor*, 1895. Watercolor on paper, 5 x 7 inches. Wallace Gallery, East Hampton, New York.

41. Alfred Thompson Bricher (1837-1908), *In My Neighbor's Garden*, 1883. Oil on canvas, 24 x 44 inches. Collection of Hirschl and Adler Galleries, New York City.

42-43. Jessie Tarbox Beals, *The Apple Trees*, Southampton, Mr. & Mrs. Henry E. Coe, 1915. Photograph in *Beautiful Gardens in America* by Louise Shelton.

Photographer unknown, *The Apple Trees*, Southampton, Mr. & Mrs. Henry E. Coe, ca. 1925. Archives of American Gardens, Garden Club of America Collection, Smithsonian Institution, Washington, D.C.

44. Theodore Wores, *Thomas Moran's Garden*, 1894-1900. Oil on canvas, 12 x 8 inches. Wallace Gallery, East Hampton, New York.

45. Thomas Moran in the garden of The Studio, late 1890s. Albumen print, 4¼ x 3 inches. Guild Hall Museum, East Hampton, New York.

Theodore Wores (1858–1939), *Thomas Moran's House (East Hampton, Long Island)*, 1894-1900. Oil on board, 9 x 12 inches. Collection of Drs. Ben and A. Jess Shenson, whereabouts unknown.

46. Annette Parmentier Moran (1862–1935), *The Garden Walk (Mary Nimmo Moran Tending Her Garden)*, 1881. Oil on canvasboard, 17 x 14 inches. Wallace Gallery, East Hampton, New York.

47. Mary Nimmo Moran (1842–1899), *Dr. E. Osborne's Garden*, 1895. Oil on canvas 19¾ x 15½ inches. Long Island Collection, East Hampton Free Library, New York.

49. Mattie Edwards Hewitt, *James Lawrence Breese Estate*, ca. 1920. Albumen print, 10 x 8 inches. Nassau County Museum, Long Island Studies Institute, Hempstead, New York.

50. McKim, Mead, and White, *Plan and Elevation for the Residence of James Lawrence Breese, Southampton, Long Island, New York*, 1906.

51. Miss Johnston-Mrs. Hewitt, *The Orchard, Southampton, Long Island, Mr. and Mrs. James Lawrence Breese*, 1915. Photographs in *Beautiful gardens of America*, by Louise Shelton.

52. Walter Cole Brigham, *Poor Gardens, Shelter Island*, ca. 1935. Oil on canvasboard, 5 x 7 inches. Wallace Gallery, East Hampton, New York.

53. Walter Cole Brigham, *Poor Gardens, Shelter Island*, ca. 1935. Oil on canvasboard, 5 x 7 inches. Wallace Gallery, East Hampton, New York.

54-55. Mattie Edwards Hewitt, *Barberryland, Southampton, Long Island, Mr. and Mrs. Charles Sabin*, 1915. Photographs in *Beautiful Gardens in America* by Louise Shelton.

56. Samuel H. Gottscho, *H. H. Rogers', Jr. Estate, Black Point*. Albumen prints, ca. 1920, Southampton Historical Museum, Southampton, New York.

57. Florence Vincent Robinson (1874–1916), *Lily Pond at Black Point*, ca. 1919. Watercolor on paper, 15 x 22⅛ inches, Southampton Historical Museum, Southampton, New York.

58. Gaines Ruger Donoho (1857–1937), *Woodhouse Water Garden*, 1911. Oil on canvas, 24 x 34 inches. Guild Hall Museum, East Hampton, New York; gift of Mrs. Lorenzo Woodhouse.

59. Childe Hassam, *The [Woodhouse] Water Garden*, 1909. Oil on canvas, 24 x 36 inches. Metropolitan Museum of Art, New York City; part and partial gift of Mr. and Mrs. Douglas Dillon.

60-61. Miss Johnston-Mrs. Hewitt, *Virginia Kent Cummings Water Garden*. Albumen print, 1914. Long Island Collection, East Hampton Free Library, East Hampton, New York.

62. Caroline M. Bell (1874-1970), *Iris Garden*, ca. 1930. Oil on board, 15¼ x 18½ inches. Wallace Gallery, East Hampton, New York.

63. Miss Johnston-Mrs. Hewitt, *Mrs. Lorenzo Woodhouse (The Fens) East Hampton*, 1915. Hand-colored glass lantern slide photograph. Archives of American Gardens, Garden Club of America Collection, Smithsonian Institution, Washington, D.C.

65. Gaines Ruger Donoho, *Path to The Studio*, 1890–1916. Oil on canvas, 30 x 36 inches. Collection of Hirschl and Adler Galleries, New York City.

66-67. Mattie Edwards Hewitt, *Crossways, the Garden of Willim Wallace Benjamin. Garden of the Pruyn Sisters*, East Hampton, New York. Photographs, ca. 1925. Nassau County Museum, Long Island Studies Institute, Hemstead, New York.

68. *Albert and Adele Herter's Circular Garden at The Creeks*, photograph, ca. 1925. Nassau County Museum, Long Island Studies Institute, Hempstead, New York.

69. Albert Herter, The Creeks, East Hampton, New York, ca. 1920s. Hand-colored glass lantern slide photograph. Archives of American Gardens, Garden Club of America Collection, Smithsonian Institution, Washington, D.C.

70. Frances Benjamin Johnston, *The "garden of the moon" at The Creeks*, autochrome, 1927. In *Beautiful Gardens of America* by Louise Shelton.

71. Frances Benjamin Johnston, The Creeks, East Hampton, New York, Albert and Adele Herter, 1915. In *Beautiful Gardens of America* by Louise Shelton.

72-73. Linda Alpern, *Ossorio's Garden, The Creeks*, 1989. Collection of the photographer.

74. Alfonso Ossorio, *Swimming Pool at the Creeks*, 1989. Collection of Linda Alpert.

75. Linda Alpern, *The Creeks in Winter*, 1990. Collection of the photographer.

76. *Frank B. Wiborg Residence and Gardens*, ca. 1924. Hand-colored postcard. Long Island Collection, East Hampton Free Library, East Hampton, New York.

77. Mattie Edwards Hewitt, *The Wiborg Garden with View of Hook Pond*, photograph, ca. 1924. Nassau County Museum, Long Island Studies Institute, Hempstead, New York.

Frances Benjamin Johnston, *Circular Pond at the Wiborg Residence, East Hampton, New York*, ca. 1920s. Hand-colored glass lantern slide photograph. Archives of American Gardens, Garden Club of America Collection, Smithsonian Institution, Washington, D.C.

78-79. *Anna Gilman Hill's Gray Garden*, ca. 1925. Hand-colored glass lantern slide photograph. Archives of American Gardens, Garden Club of America Collection, Smithsonian Institution, Washington, D.C.

81. Mattie Edwards Hewitt, *Anna Gilman Hill's Gray Garden*, photograph, 1923. Nassau County Museum, Long Island Studies Institute, Hempstead, New York.

82-83. Mattie Edwards Hewitt, *Anna Gilman Hill's Excedra and Thatched Tool Shed*, and *Mrs. Hill's Rose-encrusted Excedra*, photographs, 1923. Nassau County museum, Long Island Studies Institute, Hempstead, New York.

84. *Ruth Dean Garden at Guild Hall, East Hampton, New York*, photograph, 1932. Aymar Embury II architectural plan for Guild Hall Museum, East Hampton, New York, 1930. Guild Hall Museum Collection.

Childe Hassam, *The Guild Hall, East Hampton*, 1931. Etching, $6\frac{1}{2}$ x $8\frac{3}{8}$ inches. Guild Hall Museum, East Hampton, New York, Guild Hall Purchase Fund.

85. Samuel H. Gottscho, *Ruth Dean Garden Behind the East Hampton Library*, photograph 1924. Long Island Collection, East Hampton Free Library, East Hampton, New York.

94. Rachel Hartley (1884–1959). *Winter Garden in Southampton*, ca. 1930. Oil on canvas on board, 30 x 25 inches. Wallace Gallery, East Hampton, New York.

95. Rachel Hartley (1884-1959). *Summer Garden in South-ampton*, ca. 1930. Oil on board, 30 x 20 inches. Wallace Gallery, East Hampton, New York.

102. Fountain designed by Costantino Nivola for his garden in The Springs of East Hampton. Photograph from the collection of Ruth Nivola, ca. 1955.

107. Claire and Pietro Nivola playing in the Nivola garden in The Springs of East Hampton. The Nivola garden in winter. Photographs from the collection of Ruth Nivola, ca. 1955.

109. Robert Dash (1934-), *New Weather*, 1983. Oil on canvas, 70 x 60 inches. Lizan Tops Gallery, East Hampton, New York.

113. Cornelia Foss (1937-), *Summer Garden*, 2003. Oil on canvas, 30 x 42 inches. DFN Gallery, New York City.

117. Donald Sultan (1951-), *Morning Glories, July 1988*. Oil on canvas, 12 x 12 inches. Collection of Frances Sultan.

120. Ty Straudsburg (1940-), *Pond at LongHouse*, 2003. Oil on linen, 32 x 30 inches. Arlene Bujese Gallery, East Hampton, New York.

129. Roy W. Nicholson (1943-), *Gloaming Group # 5*, 2001. Acrylic and oil on linen, 48 x 48 inches. Collection of the artist, courtesy of Katarina Rich Perlow Gallery, New York City.

133. Gerson Leiber (1921-), *The Lightless Garden*, 2002. Oil on canvas, 50 x 60 inches. Denise Bibro Gallery, New York City.

135. Jennifer Bartlett (1941-), *October, Amagansett # 11*, 2002. Pastel on paper, 30 x 30 inches. Collection of the artist, courtesy of Artemis Greenberg Van Doren Gallery, New York City.

139. Jane Freilicher (1924-), *Beginning of Summer*, 1994. Oil on linen, 32¼ x 40 inches. Collection of Arnie and Elizabeth Tops Lizan, Lizan Tops Gallery, East Hampton, New York.

141. Fairfield Porter (1907-1975), *Backyards at Southampton*, 1960. Oil on linen, 30 x 20 inches. Collection: Francis A. Williams.

143. Allen Thompson Terrell (1897-1986), *Summer Flowers*, 1927. Oil on canvas, 25 x 30 inches. Wallace Gallery, East Hampton, New York.

144. Sheridan Lord (1926-1994), *Landscape April 1998-99-90-91*. Oil on canvas, 38 x 52 inches. Collection of Pamela Lord.

147. Mattie Edwards Hewitt, *Southampton Garden of Mr. and Mrs. G. Warrington Curtis*, 1914. In *Beautiful Gardens of America* by Louise Shelton.

148. Rae Ferren (1929-), *The Flowering*, 1993. Oil on canvas, 36 x 48 inches. Arlene Bujese Gallery, East Hampton, New York.

153. Nicolai Cikovsky (1894-1984), *Garden by the Sea (near Southampton)*, 1947. Oil on canvas board, 16 x 20 inches. Collection of Gary and Nina Madison, courtesy of Wallace Gallery, East Hampton, New York.

159. Mattie Edwards Hewitt, *James Lawrence Breese Estate, the Orchard*, ca. 1920. Nassau County Museum, Long Island Studies Institute, Hempstead, New York.

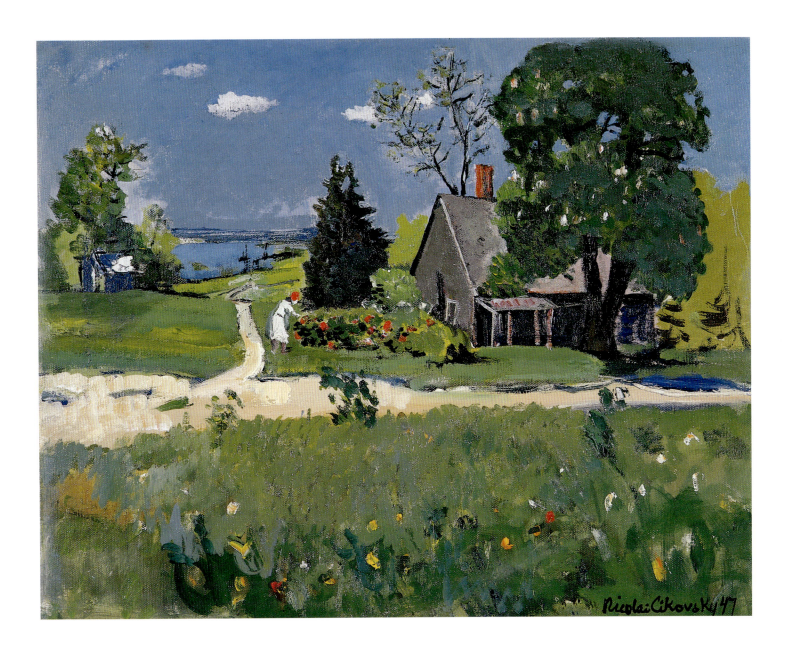

A Russian émigré, Nicolai Cikovsky, started spending summers painting in the North Sea area of Southampton beginning in 1942. By the late 1970s, he completely succumbed to the light and landscape and moved there permanently. His artist-friend Raphael Soyer observed later: "He loves moving clouds, shimmering sunlight on rippling water, and the multi-colored flowers in his own garden which he has painted so often. If one could consider painting as poetry, then Nicolai Cikovsky may be called the poet of Long Island."[23] Among the many East End pictures Cikovsky painted is *Garden by the Sea (near Southampton)*, 1947.

INDEX

For almost a century, a Doric pergola has surrounded three sides of the large formal garden at The Orchard, the colonial revival–style house designed by the prestigious architectural firm of McKim, Mead and White for Mr. and Mrs. James Lawrence Breese in Southampton. Photographed by Mattie Edwards Hewitt, ca. 1920. The Orchard was one of the twelve Long Island gardens Louise Shelton included in her extraordinary book, *Beautiful Gardens in America*, first published in 1915.

PURPLE BARBERRY